Geography of the Possible

Geography of the Possible

poems by
Susan Jackson

SHANTI ARTS PUBLISHING

BRUNSWICK, MAINE

Geography of the Possible

Published by Shanti Arts Publishing

Designed by Shanti Arts Designs

Shanti Arts LLC
193 Hillside Road
Brunswick, Maine 04011
shantiarts.com

Cover image—joe-pohle /
5XSplbkT2SM / unsplash.com

Printed in the United States of America

ISBN: 978-1-971191-09-6 (softcover)

Library of Congress Control Number: 2026937305

for my beloved parents
who gave me many doorways
into life
and for my sister, always

Contents

Acknowledgments 9

I How the House Learns To Hold Time 14
Even When I Didn't Keep Faith with the Poems 16
Ode To Compost 17
Komorebi 18
The House on Deer Run Road, Early Morning 19
Fisherman on the Bay of Banderas 20
My Life Is a Stone 21
Radiance 22
I Want My Name to Be Happiness 23
From Here to Nayarit 24
The Car Window 25
The Changing Light Through the Window 26
The Instagram Video 27
Five Strawberries on a Plate 28
Wrapping Presents 29

II Geography of the Possible 32
Ode to the Fox 33
It Was Only a Game 34
Moon Poem 35
Unexplainable 36
Introduction to Mystery 38
Yesterday and Tomorrow 40
The Evening News 41
The Empty Bench, Disappearing Days of Summer 42
Beyond 44
Where the Words Go 45
Blessing 46
October 16, 2024 47
When I Look In the Clear Mirror 49
The Invisible Letter of Love 50

III Creating a Portal 54

When Everything Is Slippery 55

The World Calls Me on My Cell Phone 56

When Something Shatters 57

The Answer Lives Inside 58

The Work We've Been Given 59

When the Creek Flows Lush and Full 60

A New Language 61

A Word Can Be a Whole Field 62

Paradox 63

Rising 64

In the Shadow of Trees 65

Where Have You Gone, Bob Dylan? 66

November 67

Quiet Is All I Have 69

Blackberries and Dark Plums 70

As Night Falls 71

To Breathe in the Night 72

Notes 75

About the Author 77

Acknowledgments

Many thanks to the editors of the following publications in which these poems first appeared:

Amethyst Review: "The Answer Lives Inside" (2025)

Earth's Daughters: "The Empty Bench, Disappearing Days of Summer" (2024)

Lily Poetry Review: "The Changing Light Through the Window" (2025)

Pensive: A Global Journal of Spirituality & the Arts: "The Car Window" (Spring 2024)

Offerings: A Spiritual Poetry Anthology of Tiferet Journal (Tiferet Press): "Even When" and "Unexplainable" [published as "What I Am Not Able To Tell"] (2022)

Tiferet Journal: "Geography of the Possible" (2025) and "When Something Shatters" [published as "After a Shattering"] (2024)

"What keeps my heart awake is colorful silence"
—Claude Monet

I

How the House Learns To Hold Time

During your illness we thought we'd feel tethered to the clock
but something else entirely happened

an hour by hour act of faith . . . you will still be here
I will still be here

eight o'clock
nine
ten o'clock
eleven

here in the chapel of hours bowing to the necessary
becomes a way of holding time and each hour as it passes

becomes a bead we thread on the long strand of our lives
these rooms we live in grow large like a wide open field

a new place we follow like a map that shows the way
through tunnels in the earth where roots sew themselves together

like us, being here with each hour; not thinking gone
as they pass or the flow leading somewhere final

or death; no, here the fullness of living in the moment leads
to a path beneath time;

now it is noon
pills then prepare our food: slice open the ripe tomato
with its fistful of seeds, the cold, crisp cucumbers into rounds

of transparent icy green and wash the leaves of lettuce;
there will be olive bread toast and tea brimming in two blue mugs

there is time for just this moment, just these hours,
what we hold onto—the bell, only the bell, and when it rings

as it should to remind me the task of nursing, when the bell rings
ripples of sound stream into the air like breath;

at some hour the stars come back, we are drowsing then,
no longer needing to steer or parse the forked places

no longer identifying time but letting the hours find me, use me
in this peculiar way they weave me into something whole

and vast like a wave that comes to know itself as ocean, as water;
the hours have not made me something other than what I am

they teach me *I am*, they have their own breath, their own rising
and falling; the bell rings, sound flows, I go to you

we find here in our own house more than we could have imagined
and for today, for right now, this abundance is enough

Even When I Didn't Keep Faith with the Poems

Even when I didn't keep faith
with the poems
they kept faith with me.
Waiting in maternity wings
by two bassinets on wheels,
while babies nursed,
as children grew;
they waited by swing sets,
in pediatrician consults,
in laundry rooms
and the garden beds; everywhere
the invisible patience of poems.
They waited by the moving van
as packing crates were lifted
and doors closed,
on the ocean liner,
and all during the war.
While chicken roasted,
while broccoli steamed, as the rice pot
overboiled. When the siren sounded,
as the ambulance arrived,
the poems kept their waiting.
January's drifting snow
and bitter wind
that somehow turned to June . . .
and all the while the poems knew.

Ode To Compost

The cat-scratch sound of the peeler moving back and forth over
the carrot's body, a growing mound of orange curl
joins the rind and seeds of two lemons in the compost pot.

Potato skins and the sticky shells of eight brown eggs cracked into
my grandmother's blue mixing bowl with the ring of flowers
around its open mouth. Red pepper core, onion husks crinkly

like ancient parchment with their history etched in invisible writing.
The still exuberant fragrance of day-old tangerine peel
that once cradled crescent moons of fruit. It all looks like chaos—

like the wings on my face that masquerade as crow's feet
and laugh lines, like the muddle of strife our world is in—
but composting takes time. Takes trust and patience.

I haul the harvest-to-be out to the heap behind the shed.
Notice fox scat on the path between the grove of spruce
and the tree stump haloed by periwinkle. The bucket feels

heavier than it should. My shoulders weighted by the news.
The violence of the world's becoming in the offices of hurt.
It's a well-worn path, this trek from kitchen to woods, to take up

the rake and churn my offerings to the earth. This is a process
that takes its own time I think as afternoon sun shimmies
on the pink and white petals of apple blossom

as if light solidified into something you could hold in your hand.
Heading back to the house I swing the empty bucket and kick
a small gray stone into the pile of sticks just for the hell of it.

Komorebi

The Japanese word

    for windy light

        through trees

I know no word

    for hard rain

        on the large flat leaves

of a sycamore tree

    or the immaculate supple

        slide into day

when dreams disappear

    and yet the invisible

        imprint of your body

against mine has not unspooled

    over time

        or has the geography of memory

morphed its boundaries

    nor lost the immeasurable warmth

        its footprint of fire

The House on Deer Run Road, Early Morning

She turns from the squat metal box
nestled in the corner between the driveway
and garage door. It is winter. As light rises
from behind the trees she realizes snow
is already falling. Her arms cradle
two glass bottles of milk, a block of butter
wrapped in gold foil. I watch her hug
this bounty to her chest in order to free
one hand long enough to brush little wheels
of frozen snow from her eye lashes.
She doesn't know I'm already up and dressed.
She doesn't feel me watching through the window
that is time and not time. I can taste the cream
I skim off the very top of the milk bottle.
I can hear the crinkle of foil unfolding.
And my father's aftershave on the air
as he pulls his chair out from the breakfast table.
How much snow are we expecting? he asks her.
I wish I knew the answer.

Fisherman on the Bay of Banderas

Waves slap the sides of the skiff.
No other sound in the deep night.
Alone in the boat he thinks
of his solitary wife asleep in their bed.
He thinks things that won't form
into words. The many years.
He knows the shape and transit
of each constellation, lets them
show him the earth's axis
and rotation, whisper the great names
Andromeda, Ursas Major and Minor,
the Dippers and Cassiopeia.
With patience he hopes the fish
are plentiful tonight. *Huachanango,*
Mahi Mahi. He thinks maybe
death is not coming so much
in darkness as held in the soft
curve of a net, cradled like his fish.

On the shore a woman looks out
from her window and sees
the single light on each boat
and thinks it looks as if the stars
have poured out of the sky
onto the surface of the water
there and there and there.

My Life Is a Stone

My life is a stone I pulled from the tide on Punta Burro Beach.
This stone lives on my desk
where far from shore it still glistens
because the stone knows what the ocean knows.
Pounded smooth, rough edges rounded
like a pocket stone
it fits my palm
the way my life never does
for the stone knows what the ocean knows
its freight an elixir of salt and cloud
this pocket stone in my palm
when I need the solace of waves
I feel its heft and weight, my time in Nayarit
like a lifeline. Because the stone knows
what the ocean knows.

Radiance

To embody the solitude of mountains
and not be afraid of the weathering storms;

to remain patient even in the vast
shuffling of wind where rivers meet at the Great Divide;

to know that yearning and remembrance are simply
the back and forward beats of one song;

then I could be alone on the empty bench outside
as if in the center of the circle of the world.

I Want My Name to Be Happiness

Pure tail-wagging-dog happiness
that welcomes everyone home.

One whose feet feel delight in the resilient
give of swamp moss on the trail.

One who knows rain, who knows night,
and when the trees extend their mighty

guardian arms to wave, let me know
them as friend, let me pause

and answer the call they call me to.
Wonder even in the chaos of our world.

I want grateful to be my middle name
and let the e enfolded in that word

stand for *enough*, let the word's quiet
buoyancy soar like a rainbow kite

splashing color across the sky
and if not a kite, let happiness

be a boat I've somehow learned
to forge from what had seemed dead

wood. A vessel to carry me in the river
that sings to the rocks and me as I dip

the long straight oar in, pull back, and
dip again, a flow, going as the water goes.

From Here to Nayarit

The garden will wait for you forever. Such patience. It knows
when you enter, hears you lift the latch, the whine of rust
as the gate swings open on its ancient hinges.
Feels your footsteps.

The hyacinths and tulips are gone. The snake said they would be.
Summer coming. The voluptuousness of peonies, all hot pink
and maroon, ready to drop their petals. White iris, with their shy
splashes of yellow, punctuate the circle, stand tall as if victorious
in some hidden skirmish of soil and rain. In the reel of change,
roses next up. Purpled by Russian sage, then the bees. Pearls of dew.
The way only stones tell the truth.

But remember Nayarit? Remember when you were hungry?
How out of the hunger came . . . what? Jaguars with wings?
They drank from well number four. They lazed in the grove
of royal palms. Ate freely of papaya, including all the black seeds,
disdained the too-sweet fruit of mango, before they flew down
from the mountain, from the *tereno*. Remember going
with them to visit parrots who lived in the nest once built
by termites? The vat of honey?
Therefore do not be afraid.

Although dead, Jose Benitez Sanchez, great shaman
of the Huichol, still walks the high path of the Sierra Madre.
Listen. He speaks through the voice of the wind. He still holds
the peyote flower in the palm of his outstretched hand. It still burns.
The scent will find you.

The Car Window

I didn't want to be the one
who left the car window open
last night. As temperatures dropped
to near freezing (the way they do
in the mountains) a car
in the driveway could be
alluring to an animal agile enough
to climb in through that window.

You're on edge my husband
told me. But the more precarious
the world feels the more the need
to be precise in the measurement
of all things: coffee beans
with a spoon. A timer for
the grinder's spin to create
the perfect texture somewhere
between powder, sand and dust.
The purity of water, the warmth
of milk. It's just mapping
infinity really.

Who is it who looks like me
watching me never knowing
what to do next. But we're all
just witnesses, right? We want
to believe the small stories
of our experience matter,
the open window,
the lost baby.
That's why I write.

The Changing Light Through the Window

My friend's son made her a gift of windows
    so from her sick bed upstairs
she could look out over the river behind her house;
    watch the blue heron swoop to fish along the bank
and across the bridge to her studio where she used to paint peonies
    and lilacs, the waterfall, portraits of children
with wide open faces.

Once in Switzerland we hiked half way up a mountain
    and paused on a bench along the path,
the sound of cow bells closer and closer and soon
    the hot breath of cows upon us . . . a herd on its way home for milking,
she and I on a hillside in the dominion of friendship,
    sun and shadow over the green patches
of land as far as we could see. Could I have thought that's how
    death comes with jangling bells and plodding hooves?

This evening her hand shapes the sheet hem as she sleeps.
    My body sinks further into the chair . . .
the changing light through the window . . . the words of Milosz
    You who I could not save / Listen to me . . .

In the ancestral lands of northern Finland some say
    when a Sami dies they become rain.
I look out this evening at the dark clouds gathering
    in the western sky and imagine being rain . . .
rain that quenches plants and trees, nourishes the living things,
    invisible until it begins falling.

The Instagram Video

No way to unsee it. The baby covered with blood
from shrapnel wounds. Trembling body.
Quiver of mouth as scant shallow breaths
snatch air in the shock of what's rained down
and if the sages say all peoples of the earth are one
then I am one with these people, with the suffering,
with this baby and I cannot turn away. Cannot want
to unsee arms of the mother blown off
from around the baby and no one left but bodies
in the stone and rubble and all I want to do is hold
this shuddering baby in my arms, somehow find a
way to soothe away the terror. This is what war does.

Five Strawberries on a Plate

The mountains have disappeared
behind morning fog or traveling smoke
from fires in California.

I can't see the hemlock
or the branches of aspen trees
as if everything familiar has become

invisible and yet the poet says infinity
is open to my sight—
I look at the five strawberries

with their green caps and stems
on the plate with scalloped edges
and think of how I went with my mother

to gather wild strawberries
from the woods in June
how she measured flour and butter

for shortcake, the whir of the beaters
as cream whipped, the clink as she stirred
in teaspoons of powdered sugar and vanilla

how she called them generous, those
dollops like clouds covering the berries
and how many years has it been now

since I was ten

Wrapping Presents

The trees this afternoon bend their branches
in the wind, they wave and caress the air
    and beckon me back

to a long ago Sunday afternoon in winter
        your touch   my left breast
    mouths   our
        unexpected pleasure rising
                with the breath inside desire

then the clamor knocking
on our bedroom door we know is closed
though probably not locked. Kids
we'd thought downstairs in the playroom
watching a rerun of *Little Women*

Go away! you shouted from the bounty of our bed
we're wrapping Christmas gifts!

and maybe only now my love
as I watch you sleeping
while the trees outside work magic
that erases time
do I begin to understand Mark Doty's words
how in poems we get to save
what in life we're not allowed to keep.

II

Geography of the Possible

The cathedral of loss death built,
    the leaded glass of its dark windows,

blew down in yesterday's wind
    making way for a small prairie.

Such is the infallible nature of nature
    to bring joy when you need it most.

I saw the miracle of a hummingbird's wings,
    those minute motorized mechanisms,

lifting its body to the nectar tucked
    inside the body of flowers. I watched

the yellow eye on an ebony bird blink
    as the bird leaned its invisible ear

to the ground listening for movement
    below the earth—the bird knelt its

way to sustenance the way some take
    a communion wafer in their cupped

hands and raise the host to their
    mouths. There are lessons abundantly

offered every day out here when I let this
    land become an inner land, a whole

geography of the possible
    opening inside me.

Ode to the Fox

Today she walks into the yard in the company of six wild turkeys
each moving with their own cadence as if conducting
a private orchestra for the patches of snow still on the ground.

She mingles, not at all aloof, while the turkeys peck at the
stubby winter grass. Hear the cluck-clucking almost more
of a cooing like your mother's voice calling your name

but it's the fox that intrigues: the way her paws move
like light, companions with the earth beneath them.
Don't you wish you could be so sure-footed, so at home

in the country that no vitality or sequence of terrain eluded you?
Nose capable of trailblazing and decoding. Permission for anything.
She comes and goes freely, will take the whole world in her mouth

to chew the juiciness without worrying what drips or spills. She simply
sows what needs to be sown and infuses the very air with grace and
the russet golden color of her fur. The white tip of her long tail.

The turkeys—she lets them go their own way.
Oh, fox.   Namaste.

It Was Only a Game

A Number 2 pencil from the Study Hotel in New Haven,
graphite probably, and sharp with a good eraser.
When she was little and fascinated by what it was to be a maker
my granddaughter and I played a game: I drew a line
or two or three and maybe a squiggle on a piece of paper.
She'd connect the lines and add her own to form a cat or a house
with windows and a chimney, sometimes smoke rose from the chimney.
She loved what she could conjure out of the paper's white sky.

Then she'd make her own few lines or half moons and hand the paper
back to me. *Now you do it, Nana.* The curves turned into eyes
on a rabbit, tendrils became butterfly wings. For hours we watched
as something from nearly nothing emerged. She bending her head
in concentration, small fingers tight on the wood of the pencil.

I didn't think at the time how life always requires connections,
teaches us to join the geometrics of disparate happenings, create
a narrative to understand as we navigate the weight and pressure,
the force of what we can't control. But how could I draw
the time between launch and landing of a missile. The silence
that comes after an air raid siren. Let explosion and silence
exist in the same picture.

My granddaughter's growing up. She knows squiggles don't
really make the mane on a horse. Circle and triangle
an ice cream cone. She's learning to draw patience
and question marks and sometimes tears.

Moon Poem

It could be resilience sent down through the women of my people
that called me out last night to look for the full moon
and remember those who came before me.

My great-grandmother birthed nine children. Five infants died.
Her mother lost three. Grandmother's story the same. When my
baby died they encircled me like an invisible force of comfort.

So today I fill a blue pottery bowl with stones for each child lost.
I place them one by one, round like the moon. The ocean made
them smooth. On each I write the name of a baby death took.

Like an incantation I say aloud *William   Mary   Sarah   John
Martin   Faith*   but the stones are hungry and porous so
the ink blurs, then disappears, letters soak into stone as if

swallowed by time. These foremothers of mine how did they
go on, walking as they did in the footprints of sorrow?
They've brought me through lineage to water and stone.

Water for remembrance and the wash of grief. Rock for
grounding and the strength of roots sent hand to hand
down the years.   *Grace*

Edwin   Henry   Hannah   the names melt
and disappear like breath in air while the stones remain
as markers for a shared grave.

Unexplainable

I'm at my desk
immersed in words

when everything around me
begins to gleam:
the writing table
with its four straight legs,
both windows and all four walls,
outpouring me
into the hall
and down the stairs . . .

is the kitchen like
this too? On the counter
the sack of new potatoes
still specked with dirt
glows with love.
Even the knotted trash
bag ready for the bin outside
lit as if some sage
had risen from her cave,
and walked in blessing
throughout our whole house.

To my surprise
I do not fall on my knees
to this profusion of presence,
if that's what it could be
called, but let it inhabit
me. Let my hands lift
one by one each
of the Idahos, scrub
and rinse their nubby skins
in cold, clear water
as if all were sacred;

then dry them
with the linen cloth,
light the stove
and begin to hum.

Introduction to Mystery

Every night in dreams
I walk a beach
where waves crash,
spray wets my face
and as I walk
I come upon a leg,
a foot, an open hand—
so many limbs collected
that I carry them like fire wood
cradled in my small arms
in search of a level place
where I can lay them down
to fit the torn off pieces
back together.

I was a child. A child dreaming
the same dream over and over.
I didn't know the word *recurring*.
I'd never heard the myth of ancient
Egypt where Osiris was dismembered,
his broken body strewn,
how Isis gathered all the parts, a wife
imbued with power to restore
her beloved husband back to life.

I know now
how dreams show life tasks,
teach us ways to reach our arms
wide, gather, sort and shape . . .
use words to build and make
and recreate . . . but the words
come from where?

Simple as blades of grass,
sweet as ripe plums,
some source accords
the braiding, binding, the kindness
of a look, line on line, page on page
this work of repair, our world.

Yesterday and Tomorrow

The child pours the boiling water from the kettle,
stirs the pot for the grandmother who is suddenly me.
How does this happen? Yesterday I was a lotus
with vermilion petals, tufted with a center of
yellow pollen, unfeckled, not knowing perfection
from rain, veil from ash. Words were the downlight
of stars, plentiful.

So, what of leaves layering under trees—
what calls them from their branches?
The force field of earth or churl of wind.
Oak and ginkgo, dogwood, plum. Deciduous
as seasons, but also skilled
in the glorious work of return.

The Evening News

Arthur asked for an apple the night he died. By the time it was washed, sliced and splayed on a white plate, carried from the kitchen to the TV room where he watched the evening news, he was gone. *No one expected it*, everyone said. Which is so often said of death. Ending the service, following the eulogies, children sang "Here Comes the Sun." Afterwards, close friends were invited to join the family for dinner at the Snake River Grill. A whole restaurant turned into the province of sorrow.

I wore black, which Renoir said is the queen of colors, and Henry hugged me beside a table in the main dining room as I offered my condolences to the widow. I tried to grasp her loss. Neither Henry nor I yet understood how much more there is to endings than coffins and dirt, for those who dare to keep their eyes open.

The long tentacles of loneliness.

The Empty Bench, Disappearing Days of Summer

From my desk I pause to gaze out the glass door
to the empty bench, as I sift through the quickly
disappearing days of summer

when my mother's presence calls me
back through space and time
to the summer I was thirteen, reading
in the family room next to her kitchen.
Ice cubes clink as she lays out
the scotch and soda my dad will drink
when he comes home from work.

The aroma as she grates cheese
over the chicken tetrazzini she has spooned
into her mother's blue crockery baking dish
with the hairline crack under the left handle.

I was never allowed to swear,
but I lay on the couch reading to her
lines from *The Catcher in the Rye* in
the voice of Holden Caufield who said *goddamn*
and maybe even the *f* word and miraculously
it was all right. She came to the doorway
to listen, a pot holder in one hand, the other
leaning against the woodland green woodwork
that framed her body like an aura
and even though I'd used the forbidden
language—Holden's language—
she looked at me with something akin
to someone arriving from another planet
where everything was different
but somehow okay—or maybe
who she saw stretched out on the woven
cushion, toes wriggling with delight,

was not her daughter but her own teenage self
unexpectedly given permission to say anything,
think anything, because after all someone had written it
in a book and set us free to be ourselves
no matter how unlikely such a possibility
might have seemed just moments before
when she lifted an ordinary casserole
and slid it onto the center rack of the preheated
375 degree stainless steel wall oven.

Beyond

when my body prickles
with bewilderment at the difficulty

of ordinary things

I look again
into the dazzling light of memory

once upon a time an otter
disappeared in the dark water
I forgot snow
and became an explorer in places
beyond the land of understanding

and for a moment everything
seemed simple, curative,
like a Damask rose, a sachet
whose fragrance lingers . . .

I was slow, curious

    invisible as air

and just as necessary

I must have been in god's eye

Where the Words Go

for Kimberly

I heard a sound like ice cracking
my daughter sobs into the phone.

After the storm her bedroom ceiling
collapsed onto where she'd been asleep

seconds before. I put down my pen
and take the first plane to Madrid.

For days we sift through rubble
like after a bomb. She weeps

because she's still alive and
it could have been

otherwise in so much debris and dust,
the many ruined things we throw away.

I go weak to think what might have been.
Muttering to no one *okay, thank you,*

thank you to praise whatever instinct
woke her, what sense drew her

to the other room. The child she was
seemed to always know the secret things.

Like the afternoon I planned to surprise
her with ice cream and as if listening

to my mind she smiled and said
I'm going to have chocolate!

Blessing

Words dowsed over me all day
and then for no reason whatsoever
I lay down on my bed
at four o'clock on a Friday
afternoon, two hands over
my heart, fingertips touching
the faithful syncopation
of beats. I slipped
out of time somehow,
every part of me at rest
and with no explanation
I could parse *forgiven*
a voice told me in an
ordinary tone of love. *You
have been good. The wanderings
and questions . . . you can let them
go now. Everything is precious.
And enough.* And I recognized
some force I could only name
a blessing as this sense of grace
washed over and through me.
Thank you were the simple words
that came. Thank you.

October 16, 2024

I notice how days sift through a calendar year,
arise with coattails of memory. Today for instance
is the birth date in 1758 of Noah Webster,

born in a clapboard house on the family farm
in West Hartford. Even as he began crawling
language came alive in his mouth.

He opted for simple, for distinguishing new country
from old. He left the English u out of honor and color,
wrote *theater* the way it sounds to the ear.

He thought the blessing of words could move the world
forward without weapons. This morning I opened
at random Noah's 1873 American Dictionary

of the English Language on my library stand,
closed my eyes and pointed to the entry for owl:
the description below the Latin name reads

"a nocturnal, carnivorous bird of short, stout form,
downy feathers, large head" with a sketch of a barn owl
above the long list of other familiars: screech owl,

great horned, saw-whet, and snowy owl.
I couldn't resist comparing the blue Dictionary app
on my iPad which describes a "chiefly nocturnal

bird of prey" then leaps to reference humans known
as night owls. *What do you think of that Noah* I say out loud . . .
2024 . . . the paltry image, the dearth of words

when suddenly   I'm face to face
with an owl at the window   dangerous eyes ablaze
in the half-light. Something shifts between us,

she and I
then they're gone—the owl
and the person I had been just one moment before.

When I Look In the Clear Mirror

for Hadewijch

The mirror turns to water
where a scarlet fish swims.
The fish knows secrets
she only tells to the dragonfly
who daily lights on the lily pad.
The lily pad sends roots in the mud
to nourish the one purple blossom
that opens to feed the ten thousand
bees who live in the dead tree
across the road. The dead tree dreams
of the life it once had.

The Invisible Letter of Love

I found the notecard in your desk drawer—
empty but for two words floating atop the swath of white:

    Dear Susan—

What did you plan to say? What were the words that dissolved
before you could pin them down on paper. What floated through

your mind, or at least the part not yet stolen by disease? Were you
going to sketch the pair of cardinals nesting in the kousa dogwood

tree beside the kitchen window . . . a riddle, a poem . . . whatever
it was, you were still alive then. I'm left with these two words so alone,

at sea as it were in the card with Eliot Porter's photo *Colorful Trees*
where it's fall, the leaves a burst of crimson with flecks of gold

on the tall, straight birch trees. And I want to know about the crimson
and gold places inside you as everything began to be eaten away.

Were you aglow like these trees in autumn, knowing
they would soon lose everything . . . were you afraid?

I love the dash—so like you whose ideas hopped and hurdled
and always reminded me of skipping stones over water, dashes

like leaps and bridges between ideas—as here,
in your last message to me that says everything without having to say

anything. I'm naming this card the *invisible letter of love.*
Your way of reaching me from the beyond.

And the dash our bond, a thread to connect us,
like a pathway always open through the woods.

This morning the sound of my pen as
it moves across the paper becomes your hand

that began to write to me,
and in the absence of words becomes

a presence tucked inside my questions
and the answers that might have been—

III

Creating a Portal

In the birch bark
eyes appear

lichen
like hair

on a sea of
faces

sounds from other
times echo

as the grove of trees
transforms

to a theater of the woods
with history's tableaux:

a white flag flies
between two men on horseback

the cherry table where
a hand scratches the words

we hold these truths
to be self-evident

on a public bus one
woman claims a place for all

the curtain once opened
can no longer be closed

When Everything Is Slippery

except the sound of gunfire and explosion
the new citizenship
bestowed on you
by the echo of emptiness
balance and rebalance both obliterated

don't expect to be in charted territory
where the zither once had seven strings
and the sun rose
between 5:45 and 6:15 each morning
count on nothing
but the ground that holds you

if the airport is destroyed
if they can't flee
let their names be written on the roster
known only to history
and those who loved them

The World Calls Me on My Cell Phone

The world calls to tell me she's lonely. Despondent. Her children bicker and sometimes worse. She's afraid one may have gotten into a bad crowd. He has a gun. She loves watching the girls run along the river, their hair sailing behind them, their shouts making the trees smile. But will they be safe, she asks herself, when the fires come? When the person who wants everyone to look alike returns to his dealmaking and delinquency.

I've loved them for so long she says. I am old and I am weary. My hope was to show them the wisdom of cycles, the letting go and rising up. What did they think the seasons were for? The moon and I, we often talk about our terrestrial and celestial messages— all the hints we've given them day in and day out, and the stars at night. I want to ask them, the world says, can't you read the augers? All I wanted was to be loved. Is that too much for a mother to hope for?

When Something Shatters

Walk the earth. Listen to the trees,
to the wisdom of seasons and forbearance.
Pummeling changes nothing.
When my baby died my mother told me
to sing to the wind. My father told me
let yourself cry. My husband held me.
The children who already imagined
themselves older sisters and brother
asked "Where is our baby?"
Like the rivers that run through
the high mountains in the Sierra Madre—
the ones you see glittering from
the airplane window—my tears flowed.
See them like a spirit gate into the cosmic map
with its topography of sorrow and joy.
The bruised heart can regrow when you
don't try to hold onto what is too heavy,
too weighted to hold. Let yourself
let go.

The Answer Lives Inside

I could tell you about this city, the rows of windows
up and down the bodies of buildings, illuminated
at night from within. All those rectangles of glass
like the lines along the fuselage of airplanes
that make me wonder who's behind them.
Who's living the secret lives inside?

Morning sun glints off the panes like a Marian apparition.
The feast day of Our Lady of Guadalupe is 12/12,
which, if you believe in the life of numbers, is double
what's needed for completion: months of a year,
a dozen eggs, the twelve signs of the Zodiac
with their individual architectures of behavior.

Our Lady gave Juan Diego a cloak of roses, emblazoned
her image on the cloth so people would believe him.

How many of us need that?

My friend told me how a child asked Agnes Martin,
"Agnes, what are your paintings about anyway?"
The artist took a rose from the vase on the table and asked,
"Is this flower beautiful?"
And the child said yes.

Agnes hid the rose behind her back. "Is the flower still
beautiful?" *Yes*, spoke the child.
"Well, that's what I paint." The power of beauty
to be present even in its absence . . .

Making the invisible visible—pulling threads
from the air and arranging them on canvas
or paper. The lines and rhythm of breath
suddenly seeable.

The Work We've Been Given

Do we near the place where women
are imprisoned in attics again?

Or can we be free to write the plays
and poems and heal the people?

How can we be holy women,
coming as we do from the lineage

of those confined by loss
and crushed hope?

We demand to know.
Perhaps we have not been angry

enough to dispel the squandered energy.
If it is not dispelled it will harm us

and our daughters and their daughters
and our sisters and our mothers.

Be willing to walk through fire.
To take our turn with courage

so the seismographic shifts
can't rupture us, so we stay true,

so the fierce one and the soft one
can be one: where we women

can find our original face
and become ourselves.

When the Creek Flows Lush and Full

Most days I sit at my desk listening for what's coming from
the other side of the air and while listening I glance outside

my window at the empty bench which is made of wood but
looks as if stitched together with cloth and thread so soft and

brown as a fresh bagel, like comfort, or those ice-cold fudgesicles
we'd buy from Foremost Dairy on the way home from dance class

when I was nine and aren't we all on our way home from something
or other, searching for accrued kindness or like today when

the creek flows lush and full after last night's heavy rain, the sound
of water flowing through the grasses or maybe it's the wind

ruffling the aspen leaves as if it's Rumi's reed song I hear, as if
I could rest in the knowing it's all one song, even my longing,

and I begin to see my solitude like a meadow full of
coneflowers abuzz with bees

A New Language

I've been ambushed by words
the same way I've been ambushed by joy:
the way wind swooshes through trees
makes words grow out of the air
the way after a night of rain
mushrooms have their thirst quenched
and rise up out of the earth.

Love is like that too—eyes say silent
things without words and hands write
eloquent soliloquies over bodies
because language is only thought made manifest
and in our private dialect, yours and mine,
the kind of storytelling we share has no need
of being bound in a book
that tries to explain soft beams of moonlight
still cast over our bed in early morning.

A Word Can Be a Whole Field

after reading "A Single Word Can Brighten the Face"
by Yunus Emre

A word can be a whole field
in which two horses cavort in the tall grass
galloping and running until grown tired
of running they come to each other
right there in the center of openness—
see how the chestnut mare nuzzles
her entire face into the free-flying mane
of the other, moves her whole prismatic
body against his.

                And it doesn't
even have to be only two horses
alone in the word-field. You can find
goshawks and foxes with kits to feed.
Butterflies like swallowtails
and gatekeepers stir up the air
inside the word. Let the word
that is a whole field
bathe you in its honey light,
loosen even the heaviest barbs
that pierce as if stitched
to your soul.

In such a pause the word radiates
off the ground, up toward
the archipelago of clouds
in the sky sea and beyond
and the word is holy, holy.

Paradox

the day my father died

I was awakened before dawn

by a great kindness

entering the room

the phone call came

I knew

must come

my sister saying

he's gone

but how

can that be true?

Rising

The fortune teller did not predict it.
The moon with her wide eye could not see it.
What was written in those letters? I tell you
I remember everything, but I lie.
I remember sticks floating downstream,
those flimsy boats. I remember the light on my hand
as I tossed them off the embankment.
Was it reckless?
Macfarlane says *language is used not only to navigate*
but also to charm the land. And indeed the wind bowed the
grasses.
And the song of the stars too.
Was I charmed?

Impossible to know—
memories rise like smoke
into sky and become the blue beyond.

On the raised hearth we used to leave dough to rise on the warm
brick, loaves wrapped in dish towels patterned with daisies
and green trees. Dough baked in the oven became bread.
That was innocence. I did not realize how easily all is lost.
Forgive me.

In the Shadow of Trees

we follow the footpath along the stream

    somewhat breathless now

and then beyond the trees we turn as the path turns

    into a field of wildflowers

and I gasp—the dazzle of columbine,

    profusion of purple lupine and alpine daisies

but what grabs me by the throat

    are the thousand petaled yellow blossoms I can't name

only remember van Gogh called *yellow a color that could charm God.*

    What is it about light and color?

My body once thought any question could be answered

    by the silence of night and your body. To sleep and dream

entwined . . . be like the hidden things

    restored in darkness

like lava and mushrooms, a new moon . . . who says light

    is the only thing capable of beguiling happiness

to come out in the open. After all,

    what about love?

Where Have You Gone, Bob Dylan?

With twang and a harmonica
the title of your next ballad
could have been faith
but you know the Jack of Hearts
has long ago left town
and perhaps it's too late
to be lonesome now
when there's blood
on the tracks
and no shelter
from the storm—
maybe just a simple
twist of fate
but oh Mama, do I have to ask again
if this can *really* be the end . . .
but know the answer is only blowin' in the wind

November

One red apple still hangs
from the craggy center branch
of an eighty-year-old apple tree.

It's November. All the leaves have fallen off.
Two frosts come and gone
and still one remaining fruit

where once an orchard
filled our back field.
I text a photo to the kids.

Brave little apple one replies. *Save the seeds*
another answers. *There's longevity*
in its DNA. Let's plant a whole new tree.

On Instagram someone posts
a picture of Henri Matisse propped up
on pillows, one hand holds

a long thin stick
like a divining rod he's using
to draw pictures on the wall beside his bed.

The caption says *Undiscourageable.*
The artist must create though age
and infirmity have overtaken him,

he's still in conversation with the world he loves.
So let me not languish. Let me persevere
the vagaries and temporality of weather:

hold fast, reach and marvel—
that last apple, this artist . . . let
the state of wonder carry me

right over the next threshold, over
the long glorious bridge
into whatever comes next.

Quiet Is All I Have

Quiet and moonlight. How can I complain that the moon is so bright
it's hard to see the meteor showers except in my mind's eye.
I can imagine flashes striating the sky, accept the memory
of other cold December nights in exchange for this one.
I glance over to where shadows jig across the moonlit grass
and there a small red fox pauses to sniff the winter air
then, phantom-like, disappears into the temple of trees.
Quiet is almost all I have. Quiet and moonlight.
And a red fox.

Blackberries and Dark Plums

It was the year of the revolution.
Tanks rolled through the city streets
and we felt at sea in a country not born as ours.
Our telephone was tapped. Mail arrived unsealed,
shamelessly opened and read. Americans here
were up to no good they said. We stood on the
Western-most point of Europe where the ocean
winds whipped at our faces. The children
played on the beach oblivious to the hidden forces
at work. In the evenings we drank wine with
the fragrance of blackberries and dark plums,
like liquid fruit from the Alentejo as we waited
to see which way things would go. People wrote
fado and sang the rhythm of life's sorrows
in a tavern at the top of a hill. All through that year
of living in the unknown we learned new words
like *leite* for milk, *estrelas* are stars, *medo* means fear
in the language new on our tongues. We took
Flipper the golden lab on long walks, threw sticks
for her to chase and bound back with.
We kept two suitcases packed and stashed
in the hall closet by the front door in case word came
it was time to flee. Some things settle at their own
pace, in their own time. This is all a memory
now, but we know what impossible futures look
like for too many people. What the world allows
to happen in its storm-driven house.

As Night Falls

and time races through our lives like water covers land,
when the cry of the hawk is no longer heard and the moon hides
    itself
behind clouds

                  even now, even still,
    I can see my mother, dead all these years, see her at the
    kitchen sink
holding a sieve in one hand and with the other
pouring a turquoise pannier of blueberries
onto the mesh. I hear the rush and splash of water
and watch her shake the berries
like a handful of jewels she turns out onto
a dish towel to dry. The griddle is already hot.
The batter made. From the table what sizzles hits
 our noses even before our ears.

It is Saturday morning. It is the ritual of family
and the short stack of blueberry pancakes
my mother is about to offer me on a white plate
with its aureole of trees. She'll touch my shoulder
as she leans in to kiss me. Though the years are all gone now,
gobbled the way my sister and I devoured mouthfuls
drenched in Vermont maple syrup, though night is falling
over and over, I welcome the whole house still alive inside me.

And if none of this makes sense to you go outside and let the stars
    explain.

To Breathe in the Night

On the day you died I was in another state,

husband in surgery, anxious voices of our children on the phone.

Thinking I wanted darkness and quiet I walked outside

to breathe in the night, mesmerized by the silence

when you spoke. *I'm free* your voice said. *It's more amazing*

than you could ever imagine. If people only knew they would

never be afraid again. I took a deep, deep breath. Didn't ask

myself is this possible, is this real? I had never in my life been

less in need of answering those questions. There was

a message here, whether spoken by the night air, the far

away stars—I took the message in both hands and held it to

my chest in a state of awe. Are there things we cannot know?

I know I felt your presence here and there, wherever there might

be. I thought of how friendship moves in a circle. Our circle

wasn't gone. It's simply way bigger than I thought it could be.

That night I dream your house is being sold and wonder where

you will live now. I dream a woman is telling me the story

of an inextinguishable light that lives inside of everyone.

Notes

[18] *"Komorebi"*— *Komorebi* is a Japanese word that literally translated means "sunlight leaking through trees," like dappled light through tree branches and leaves.

[26] "The Changing Light Through the Window"— The line "You who I could not save / Listen to me . . . " is from "Dedication" by Czeslaw Milosz, translated by the poet (Warsaw, 1945).

[29] "Wrapping Presents"— The last lines are (I think) from Mark Doty, though I can't be completely sure. I asked Mark, who didn't remember saying it but thought he might have said it, and, if so, as an ad lib remark.

[49] "When I Look in the Clear Mirror"— The dedication "for Hadewijch" references the poem "You who want . . . " by Hadewijch II, translated by Jane Hirshfield, *Women in Praise of the Sacred*, Harper Collins, 1994.

[62] "A Word Can Be a Whole Field"— This poem references "A Single Word Can Brighten the Face" by Yunus Emre, translated by Kabir Helminski and Refik Algan.

[64] "Rising"— The Robert Macfarlane reference is from *Landmarks*, Penguin Paperback 2016 Edition, page 22.

[66] "Where Have You Gone Bob Dylan?"— References are made to several Dylan songs, including "Lily, Rosemary and the Jack of Hearts," "You're Gonna Make Me Lonesome When You Go," "Shelter From the Storm," and "Simple Twist of Fate" from the 1975 album *Blood on the Tracks;* "Stuck Inside of Mobile with the Memphis Blues Again" from *Blonde on Blonde*, 1966; and the last line refers to "Blowing in the Wind," 1962.

And With Thanks

To Christine Cote and all the team at Shanti Arts Publishing.

With appreciation for the beloved community of Wednesday afternoon poets, the sensibilities and insights of Raechel Bratnick, Donna Baier Stein, Leigh Rosoff, Alexander Levering Kern, Deborah Leipziger, Ruth Dickey, Nicole Callihan, Linda Gager, and especially to John, always my first reader. To my daughters Alexandra, Kimberly, and Jennifer for their grace and guidance, and to my son, Don, for his unfailing wit and wisdom.

Thanks to the many dear friends who bring me deeper into poetry every day.

To Poets & Writers, the Academy of American Poets, the Poetry Society of America, the National Book Foundation, Tiferet for their dedication to inspiring the wide community of writers.

With gratitude to the New Jersey State Council on the Arts, the Geraldine R. Dodge Foundation, the Virginia Center for the Creative Arts, and the Vermont Studio Center.

And to you dear readers.

 SUSAN JACKSON was born in Atlanta, Georgia, and grew up in the family's native Connecticut. She lived in France, Belgium, Portugal, and Holland before settling in New Jersey where she practiced a number of healing modalities including Jin Shin Jyutsu and Nondual healing. She is the author of two previous poetry collections, *Through a Gate of Trees* and *In the River of Songs*, as well as the chapbook *All the Light in Between*. Jackson's poems have been published in literary journals including *Tiferet, Lily Poetry Review, Pensive*, and others. She and her husband, John, are the parents of four grown children and now live in Teton County, Wyoming. Find her on Instagram at susanjacksonpoet.

Shanti Arts

Nature · Art · Spirit

Please visit us online
to browse our entire book catalog,
including poetry collections and
non-fiction books on nature, healing,
art, and more.

Also take a look at our highly
regarded art and literary journal,
Still Point Arts Quarterly, a feast for
the eyes and the imagination —
available to download for free.

www.shantiarts.com

www.ingramcontent.com/pod-product-compliance
Lightning Source LLC
Chambersburg PA
CBHW051007050726
47592CB00007B/2736